ANXIETY JOURNAL

Record,
Analyse,
Manage.

Olga Gibbs

Raging Bear Publishing

Anxiety Journal.

Published in 2020 by Raging Bear Publishing.

The journal is published as a resource and guide intended to educate the reader
on what they can do to improve their anxiety, aiding a better management of the
condition. The provided information is not meant to replace a guidance or advice of a
mental health professional.

Paperback ISBN 978-1-9164710-4-7

INTRODUCTION

Anxiety refers to multiple mental and physiological phenomena, including a person's conscious state of worry over a future unwanted event, or fear of an actual situation (Evans et al, "Treating and preventing adolescent mental health disorders", Oxford Medicine). Some researchers define anxiety simply as "inability to regulate emotions", whilst others tie anxiety with an error-related brain activity.

But irrespective of the definition, all health experts agree that understanding anxieties is the first step in managing them.

Anxiety can be a crippling mental health issue to live with. It can affect our day-to-day living, enjoyment of life and can have negative effect on professional life, self-esteem, personal life, relationships and social interaction.

CBT (Cognitive Behavioural Therapy) has been deemed to deliver the best results in anxiety management. CBT focuses on how thoughts, beliefs and attitudes affect our feelings and subsequent behaviour. CBT aims to stop negative thoughts cycles by breaking them down and making problems more manageable. CBT helps to change the negative thought pattern, to analyse anxieties and its triggers by finding thought or situational patterns.

Usually, in CBT you will be working with a therapist to identify those patterns of thought and behaviour, but ultimately, once you have identified those thoughts and behaviours, you can challenge them and in turn change the way you feel in certain situations, managing and changing your behavioural response to those situations in future.

As much as all types of journaling, including gratitude journaling, have been found to be very beneficial in managing anxieties, this journal has been developed especially with anxieties management in mind.

This journal holds two sets of anxiety developed questionnaires, with questions designed to understand your anxieties, conditions and situations, during which they occurred, then analysing the outcome of each episode.

The questionnaire for each anxiety episode is then supported by a gratitude prompt, to end the episode and its evaluation on a positive note.

By analysing anxieties and its triggers, this journal provides you with a deeper understanding of your mental health condition, discovering repetition in triggers, conditions and situations, thus future-proofing your anxiety management by changing your behavioural response to anxiety episodes.

WHY ANXIETY JOURNAL?

Journaling is a highly recommended stress management tool. The benefits of journaling on mental health are well documented. Processing your emotions on paper can be helpful in managing a range of mental health conditions. Numerous studies have demonstrated the effectiveness of journaling for health, happiness and stress management, including managing anxiety. Not only is it a simple technique, it is an invaluable tool for introspection, better understanding of self and mental health condition.

There are many ways to journal. You can add a journaling habit to your life whether you journal daily, weekly, or as this journal is intended, on an as needed basis when stress and anxiety become too intense.

Understanding anxiety is the first step in managing it. In knowing its erratic nature, we can obtain a better sense of triggering situations and how our anxiety operates. Left unchecked, anxiety can lead to stress and rumination. Some of the roots of your anxiety can be minimized through focused examination.

This anxiety journal will assist you in examining and shifting thoughts from anxious and ruminative to empowered and action-oriented.

This journal, with self-analysing prompts will help you to write yourself out of stress and anxiety by better understanding your anxiety and its triggers, while providing management and relief techniques, and it will take only a few minutes of your day.

This journal is developed on the "Action-Focused Journaling" technique. It will assist you in putting your worries and concerns to paper, examining and investigating them, while finding a pattern, then reflecting, and finally exiting smart – armed with knowledge, with coping strategies and better understanding of yourself.

HOW TO RECORD.

This journal is designed to provide you with a space to record, evaluate and understand your anxieties. It holds forty pages of daily anxiety records, forty pages of gratitude journal as well, both as tools for confronting and understanding your anxiety.

We are providing you with two ways to record your anxieties: a daily log with prompt questions and a daily log, arranged as a table, and there are twenty of each. Please use both, note your responses and discover which type of anxiety journaling works best for you.

Carry this journal with you, record in it every time you experience anxiety. Write freely and honestly. Don't be afraid to sound "silly" or "overreacting" – this is your private space.

TREATMENT OF ANXIETY WITH CBT:

1. Psych-education – understanding what anxiety is and how it affects you.
2. Challenging negative thoughts – acknowledge of thoughts contributing to anxiety, whilst putting fears into perspective.
3. Exposure therapy – exposure to a source of anxiety.
4. Relaxation skills – personal techniques that initiating a calming response.

MY ANXIETY LOOKS LIKE THIS:

This space is for you to look deeper into your mind and release the grip of your self-conciseness. Let your body and mind to take over. Feel free to doodle, use different colours, or scribble. There is no wrong way to explore your anxiety.

WHEN ANXIETY COMES,
IT FEELS LIKE THIS:

This is your free writing exercise to investigate what effect anxiety has on your body, so that you can work on controlling your body, thus controlling anxiety.

50 THINGS THAT MAKE ME ANXIOUS OR STRESSED:

There's no rush to write these all at once. Make this list during your period of journaling. Understanding anxiety triggers is the first step in managing anxiety.

50 THINGS THAT MAKE ME HAPPY:

You don't have to complete this list in one go. Take your time. Reflect.
Understanding your happy spaces will provide you with coping mechanisms.

Meditation is the key!

Anxiety is a cognitive state connected to an inability to regulate emotions. But research shows that consistent meditation practice reprograms neural pathways in the brain and therefore, improves our ability to regulate emotions.

Use the table below to rate your anxiety level from 1 to 10 (1 is calm and 10 is very anxious) before and after meditation, noting the length of meditation. Find your favourite meditation technique or just sit in a quiet room, listening to your own heartbeat, being in the moment.

Should you have severe anxiety, or if you've been diagnosed with an anxiety disorder, always speak to a health care professional to talk through your options and figure out how to make meditation a component of your overall treatment program.

Date	How long did you meditate?	How did you feel before meditation?	How did you feel after meditation?

The moments of happiness

There has been extensive research connecting gratitude journaling with improvement in mental health. The long-term benefits of concentrating on positivity are well documented, and we are going to look for rays of sunshine in otherwise dark stormy skies. We need to learn to look for positivity in otherwise ordinary or challenging days, so note here something positive. Did someone say something nice to you, give a compliment or say that they love you? Maybe someone picked up a glove hat you dropped or simply smiled at you? No matter how small, note these little rays of sunshine here.

Date	What positive moment had happened?	Had you noticed it at that time?	Would you spot a similar positive moment in the future?

ANXIETY RECORDS

DATE:

Why am I worried today?

How severe is my anxiety today? (Mark it from 1 to 10, where 1 is being calm and 10 is being very anxious)

What am I thinking?

What's the proof that it will happen?

What's the proof that it won't happen?

So what if it happens?

How can I deal with it?

What can I say and do to help me get through this?

OUTCOME

Please record if your fears came true. What was the outcome of that anxiety episode? Were you right to worry? Be honest.

LET'S GIVE GRATITUDE!

List three things that you've enjoyed today or which made you happy, no matter how small. We need to see that even in anxiety-filled days we have something to be thankful for.

1.

2.

3.

ANXIETY RECORDS

DATE:
Why am I worried today?

How severe is my anxiety today? (Mark it from 1 to 10, where 1 is being calm and 10 is being very anxious)

What am I thinking?

What's the proof that it will happen?

What's the proof that it won't happen?

So what if it happens?

How can I deal with it?

What can I say and do to help me get through this?

OUTCOME
Please record if your fears came true. What was the outcome of that anxiety episode? Were you right to worry? Be honest.

LET'S GIVE GRATITUDE!

List three things that you've enjoyed today or which made you happy, no matter how small. We need to see that even in anxiety-filled days we have something to be thankful for.

1.

2.

3.

ANXIETY RECORDS

DATE:
Why am I worried today?

How severe is my anxiety today? (Mark it from 1 to 10, where 1 is being calm and 10 is being very anxious)

What am I thinking?

What's the proof that it will happen?

What's the proof that it won't happen?

So what if it happens?

How can I deal with it?

What can I say and do to help me get through this?

OUTCOME

Please record if your fears came true. What was the outcome of that anxiety episode? Were you right to worry? Be honest.

LET'S GIVE GRATITUDE!

List three things that you've enjoyed today or which made you happy, no matter how small. We need to see that even in anxiety-filled days we have something to be thankful for.

1.

2.

3.

ANXIETY RECORDS

DATE:

Why am I worried today?

How severe is my anxiety today? (Mark it from 1 to 10, where 1 is being calm and 10 is being very anxious)

What am I thinking?

What's the proof that it will happen?

What's the proof that it won't happen?

So what if it happens?

How can I deal with it?

What can I say and do to help me get through this?

OUTCOME

Please record if your fears came true. What was the outcome of that anxiety episode? Were you right to worry? Be honest.

LET'S GIVE GRATITUDE!

List three things that you've enjoyed today or which made you happy, no matter how small. We need to see that even in anxiety-filled days we have something to be thankful for.

1.

2.

3.

ANXIETY RECORDS

DATE:
Why am I worried today?

How severe is my anxiety today? (Mark it from 1 to 10, where 1 is being calm and 10 is being very anxious)

What am I thinking?

What's the proof that it will happen?

What's the proof that it won't happen?

So what if it happens?

How can I deal with it?

What can I say and do to help me get through this?

OUTCOME
Please record if your fears came true. What was the outcome of that anxiety episode? Were you right to worry? Be honest.

LET'S GIVE GRATITUDE!

List three things that you've enjoyed today or which made you happy, no matter how small. We need to see that even in anxiety-filled days we have something to be thankful for.

1.

2.

3.

ANXIETY RECORDS

DATE:
Why am I worried today?

How severe is my anxiety today? (Mark it from 1 to 10, where 1 is being calm and 10 is being very anxious)

What am I thinking?

What's the proof that it will happen?

What's the proof that it won't happen?

So what if it happens?

How can I deal with it?

What can I say and do to help me get through this?

OUTCOME

Please record if your fears came true. What was the outcome of that anxiety episode? Were you right to worry? Be honest.

LET'S GIVE GRATITUDE!

List three things that you've enjoyed today or which made you happy, no matter how small. We need to see that even in anxiety-filled days we have something to be thankful for.

1.

2.

3.

ANXIETY RECORDS

DATE:
Why am I worried today?

How severe is my anxiety today? (Mark it from 1 to 10, where 1 is being calm and 10 is being very anxious)

What am I thinking?

What's the proof that it will happen?

What's the proof that it won't happen?

So what if it happens?

How can I deal with it?

What can I say and do to help me get through this?

OUTCOME

Please record if your fears came true. What was the outcome of that anxiety episode? Were you right to worry? Be honest.

LET'S GIVE GRATITUDE!

List three things that you've enjoyed today or which made you happy, no matter how small. We need to see that even in anxiety-filled days we have something to be thankful for.

1.

2.

3.

ANXIETY RECORDS

DATE:
Why am I worried today?

How severe is my anxiety today? (Mark it from 1 to 10, where 1 is being calm and 10 is being very anxious)

What am I thinking?

What's the proof that it will happen?

What's the proof that it won't happen?

So what if it happens?

How can I deal with it?

What can I say and do to help me get through this?

OUTCOME

Please record if your fears came true. What was the outcome of that anxiety episode? Were you right to worry? Be honest.

LET'S GIVE GRATITUDE!

List three things that you've enjoyed today or which made you happy, no matter how small. We need to see that even in anxiety-filled days we have something to be thankful for.

1.

2.

3.

ANXIETY RECORDS

DATE:
Why am I worried today?

How severe is my anxiety today? (Mark it from 1 to 10, where 1 is being calm and 10 is being very anxious)

What am I thinking?

What's the proof that it will happen?

What's the proof that it won't happen?

So what if it happens?

How can I deal with it?

What can I say and do to help me get through this?

OUTCOME

Please record if your fears came true. What was the outcome of that anxiety episode? Were you right to worry? Be honest.

LET'S GIVE GRATITUDE!

List three things that you've enjoyed today or which made you happy, no matter how small. We need to see that even in anxiety-filled days we have something to be thankful for.

1.

2.

3.

ANXIETY RECORDS

DATE:

Why am I worried today?

How severe is my anxiety today? (Mark it from 1 to 10, where 1 is being calm and 10 is being very anxious)

What am I thinking?

What's the proof that it will happen?

What's the proof that it won't happen?

So what if it happens?

How can I deal with it?

What can I say and do to help me get through this?

OUTCOME

Please record if your fears came true. What was the outcome of that anxiety episode? Were you right to worry? Be honest.

LET'S GIVE GRATITUDE!

List three things that you've enjoyed today or which made you happy, no matter how small. We need to see that even in anxiety-filled days we have something to be thankful for.

1.

2.

3.

The reflection corner

Please use this page to reflect on the last ten anxiety episodes.

Using free writing, look back, evaluate them, noting your "low points" (when you were stressed the most), whilst remembering to mention the "high", happy moments within the same timeframe.

ANXIETY RECORDS

DATE:

Why am I worried today?

How severe is my anxiety today? (Mark it from 1 to 10, where 1 is being calm and 10 is being very anxious)

What am I thinking?

What's the proof that it will happen?

What's the proof that it won't happen?

So what if it happens?

How can I deal with it?

What can I say and do to help me get through this?

OUTCOME

Please record if your fears came true. What was the outcome of that anxiety episode? Were you right to worry? Be honest.

LET'S GIVE GRATITUDE!

List three things that you've enjoyed today or which made you happy, no matter how small. We need to see that even in anxiety-filled days we have something to be thankful for.

1.

2.

3.

ANXIETY RECORDS

DATE:

Why am I worried today?

How severe is my anxiety today? (Mark it from 1 to 10, where 1 is being calm and 10 is being very anxious)

What am I thinking?

What's the proof that it will happen?

What's the proof that it won't happen?

So what if it happens?

How can I deal with it?

What can I say and do to help me get through this?

OUTCOME

Please record if your fears came true. What was the outcome of that anxiety episode? Were you right to worry? Be honest.

LET'S GIVE GRATITUDE!

List three things that you've enjoyed today or which made you happy, no matter how small. We need to see that even in anxiety-filled days we have something to be thankful for.

1.

2.

3.

ANXIETY RECORDS

DATE:

Why am I worried today?

How severe is my anxiety today? (Mark it from 1 to 10, where 1 is being calm and 10 is being very anxious)

What am I thinking?

What's the proof that it will happen?

What's the proof that it won't happen?

So what if it happens?

How can I deal with it?

What can I say and do to help me get through this?

OUTCOME

Please record if your fears came true. What was the outcome of that anxiety episode? Were you right to worry? Be honest.

LET'S GIVE GRATITUDE!

List three things that you've enjoyed today or which made you happy, no matter how small. We need to see that even in anxiety-filled days we have something to be thankful for.

1.

2.

3.

ANXIETY RECORDS

DATE:
Why am I worried today?

How severe is my anxiety today? (Mark it from 1 to 10, where 1 is being calm and 10 is being very anxious)

What am I thinking?

What's the proof that it will happen?

What's the proof that it won't happen?

So what if it happens?

How can I deal with it?

What can I say and do to help me get through this?

OUTCOME

Please record if your fears came true. What was the outcome of that anxiety episode? Were you right to worry? Be honest.

LET'S GIVE GRATITUDE!

List three things that you've enjoyed today or which made you happy, no matter how small. We need to see that even in anxiety-filled days we have something to be thankful for.

1.

2.

3.

ANXIETY RECORDS

DATE:

Why am I worried today?

How severe is my anxiety today? (Mark it from 1 to 10, where 1 is being calm and 10 is being very anxious)

What am I thinking?

What's the proof that it will happen?

What's the proof that it won't happen?

So what if it happens?

How can I deal with it?

What can I say and do to help me get through this?

OUTCOME

Please record if your fears came true. What was the outcome of that anxiety episode? Were you right to worry? Be honest.

LET'S GIVE GRATITUDE!

List three things that you've enjoyed today or which made you happy, no matter how small. We need to see that even in anxiety-filled days we have something to be thankful for.

1.

2.

3.

ANXIETY RECORDS

DATE:

Why am I worried today?

How severe is my anxiety today? (Mark it from 1 to 10, where 1 is being calm and 10 is being very anxious)

What am I thinking?

What's the proof that it will happen?

What's the proof that it won't happen?

So what if it happens?

How can I deal with it?

What can I say and do to help me get through this?

OUTCOME

Please record if your fears came true. What was the outcome of that anxiety episode? Were you right to worry? Be honest.

LET'S GIVE GRATITUDE!

List three things that you've enjoyed today or which made you happy, no matter how small. We need to see that even in anxiety-filled days we have something to be thankful for.

1.

2.

3.

ANXIETY RECORDS

DATE:
Why am I worried today?

How severe is my anxiety today? (Mark it from 1 to 10, where 1 is being calm and 10 is being very anxious)

What am I thinking?

What's the proof that it will happen?

What's the proof that it won't happen?

So what if it happens?

How can I deal with it?

What can I say and do to help me get through this?

OUTCOME

Please record if your fears came true. What was the outcome of that anxiety episode? Were you right to worry? Be honest.

LET'S GIVE GRATITUDE!

List three things that you've enjoyed today or which made you happy, no matter how small. We need to see that even in anxiety-filled days we have something to be thankful for.

1.

2.

3.

ANXIETY RECORDS

DATE:

Why am I worried today?

How severe is my anxiety today? (Mark it from 1 to 10, where 1 is being calm and 10 is being very anxious)

What am I thinking?

What's the proof that it will happen?

What's the proof that it won't happen?

So what if it happens?

How can I deal with it?

What can I say and do to help me get through this?

OUTCOME

Please record if your fears came true. What was the outcome of that anxiety episode? Were you right to worry? Be honest.

LET'S GIVE GRATITUDE!

List three things that you've enjoyed today or which made you happy, no matter how small. We need to see that even in anxiety-filled days we have something to be thankful for.

1.

2.

3.

ANXIETY RECORDS

DATE:
Why am I worried today?

How severe is my anxiety today? (Mark it from 1 to 10, where 1 is being calm and 10 is being very anxious)

What am I thinking?

What's the proof that it will happen?

What's the proof that it won't happen?

So what if it happens?

How can I deal with it?

What can I say and do to help me get through this?

OUTCOME

Please record if your fears came true. What was the outcome of that anxiety episode? Were you right to worry? Be honest.

LET'S GIVE GRATITUDE!

List three things that you've enjoyed today or which made you happy, no matter how small. We need to see that even in anxiety-filled days we have something to be thankful for.

1.

2.

3.

ANXIETY RECORDS

DATE:
Why am I worried today?

How severe is my anxiety today? (Mark it from 1 to 10, where 1 is being calm and 10 is being very anxious)

What am I thinking?

What's the proof that it will happen?

What's the proof that it won't happen?

So what if it happens?

How can I deal with it?

What can I say and do to help me get through this?

OUTCOME
Please record if your fears came true. What was the outcome of that anxiety episode? Were you right to worry? Be honest.

LET'S GIVE GRATITUDE!

List three things that you've enjoyed today or which made you happy, no matter how small. We need to see that even in the anxiety-filled days we have something to be thankful for.

1.

2.

3.

The reflection corner

Please use this page to reflect on the last ten anxiety episodes.

Using free writing, look back, evaluate them, noting your "low points" (when you were stressed the most), whilst remembering to mention the "high", happy moments within the same timeframe.

Anxiety record sheet

Situation What are you doing? Who are you with? What has happened?	Emotions and body sensations What do you feel?	Your thoughts What do you think will happen? What are your concerns, fears? Be honest.	Managing anxiety Record the outcome of the anxiety episode. What have you done? How have you coped?

Make it future proof.

Have you learnt anything from this episode?

Have you discovered new coping strategies? Have you implemented them?

LET'S GIVE GRATITUDE!

List three things that you've enjoyed today or which made you happy, no matter how small. We need to see that even in the anxiety-filled days we have something to be thankful for.

1.

2.

3.

Anxiety record sheet

Situation What are you doing? Who are you with? What has happened?	Emotions and body sensations What do you feel?	Your thoughts What do you think will happen? What are your concerns, fears? Be honest.	Managing anxiety Record the outcome of the anxiety episode. What have you done? How have you coped?

Make it future proof.

Have you learnt anything from this episode?

Have you discovered new coping strategies? Have you implemented them?

LET'S GIVE GRATITUDE!

List three things that you've enjoyed today or which made you happy, no matter how small. We need to see that even in the anxiety-filled days we have something to be thankful for.

1.

2.

3.

Anxiety record sheet

Situation What are you doing? Who are you with? What has happened?	Emotions and body sensations What do you feel?	Your thoughts What do you think will happen? What are your concerns, fears? Be honest.	Managing anxiety Record the outcome of the anxiety episode. What have you done? How have you coped?

Make it future proof.

Have you learnt anything from this episode?

Have you discovered new coping strategies? Have you implemented them?

LET'S GIVE GRATITUDE!

List three things that you've enjoyed today or which made you happy, no matter how small. We need to see that even in the anxiety-filled days we have something to be thankful for.

1.

2.

3.

Anxiety record sheet

Date

Situation What are you doing? Who are you with? What has happened?	Emotions and body sensations What do you feel?	Your thoughts What do you think will happen? What are your concerns, fears? Be honest.	Managing anxiety Record the outcome of the anxiety episode. What have you done? How have you coped?

Make it future proof.

Have you learnt anything from this episode?

Have you discovered new coping strategies? Have you implemented them?

LET'S GIVE GRATITUDE!

List three things that you've enjoyed today or which made you happy, no matter how small. We need to see that even in the anxiety-filled days we have something to be thankful for.

1.

2.

3.

Anxiety record sheet

Situation What are you doing? Who are you with? What has happened?	Emotions and body sensations What do you feel?	Your thoughts What do you think will happen? What are your concerns, fears? Be honest.	Managing anxiety Record the outcome of the anxiety episode. What have you done? How have you coped?

Make it future proof.

Have you learnt anything from this episode?

Have you discovered new coping strategies? Have you implemented them?

LET'S GIVE GRATITUDE!

List three things that you've enjoyed today or which made you happy, no matter how small. We need to see that even in the anxiety-filled days we have something to be thankful for.

1.

2.

3.

Anxiety record sheet

Date

Situation What are you doing? Who are you with? What has happened?	Emotions and body sensations What do you feel?	Your thoughts What do you think will happen? What are your concerns, fears? Be honest.	Managing anxiety Record the outcome of the anxiety episode. What have you done? How have you coped?

Make it future proof.

Have you learnt anything from this episode?

Have you discovered new coping strategies? Have you implemented them?

LET'S GIVE GRATITUDE!

List three things that you've enjoyed today or which made you happy, no matter how small. We need to see that even in the anxiety-filled days we have something to be thankful for.

1.

2.

3.

Anxiety record sheet

Date

Situation	Emotions and	Your thoughts	Managing
What are you doing? Who are you with? What has happened?	body sensations What do you feel?	What do you think will happen? What are your concerns, fears? Be honest.	anxiety Record the outcome of the anxiety episode. What have you done? How have you coped?

Make it future proof.

Have you learnt anything from this episode?

Have you discovered new coping strategies? Have you implemented them?

LET'S GIVE GRATITUDE!

List three things that you've enjoyed today or which made you happy, no matter how small. We need to see that even in the anxiety-filled days we have something to be thankful for.

1.

2.

3.

Anxiety record sheet

Date

Situation What are you doing? Who are you with? What has happened?	Emotions and body sensations What do you feel?	Your thoughts What do you think will happen? What are your concerns, fears? Be honest.	Managing anxiety Record the outcome of the anxiety episode. What have you done? How have you coped?

Make it future proof.

Have you learnt anything from this episode?

Have you discovered new coping strategies? Have you implemented them?

LET'S GIVE GRATITUDE!

List three things that you've enjoyed today or which made you happy, no matter how small. We need to see that even in the anxiety-filled days we have something to be thankful for.

1.

2.

3.

Anxiety record sheet

Date

Situation What are you doing? Who are you with? What has happened?	Emotions and body sensations What do you feel?	Your thoughts What do you think will happen? What are your concerns, fears? Be honest.	Managing anxiety Record the outcome of the anxiety episode. What have you done? How have you coped?

Make it future proof.

Have you learnt anything from this episode?
Have you discovered new coping strategies? Have you implemented them?

LET'S GIVE GRATITUDE!

List three things that you've enjoyed today or which made you happy, no matter how small. We need to see that even in the anxiety-filled days we have something to be thankful for.

1.

2.

3.

Anxiety record sheet

Date

Situation	Emotions and body sensations	Your thoughts	Managing anxiety
What are you doing? Who are you with? What has happened?	What do you feel?	What do you think will happen? What are your concerns, fears? Be honest.	Record the outcome of the anxiety episode. What have you done? How have you coped?

Make it future proof.

Have you learnt anything from this episode?
Have you discovered new coping strategies? Have you implemented them?

LET'S GIVE GRATITUDE!

List three things that you've enjoyed today or which made you happy, no matter how small. We need to see that even in the anxiety-filled days we have something to be thankful for.

1.

2.

3.

The reflection corner

Please use this page to reflect on the last ten anxiety episodes.

Using free writing, look back, evaluate them, noting your "low points" (when you were stressed the most), whilst remembering to mention the "high", happy moments within the same timeframe.

Anxiety record sheet

Date

Situation What are you doing? Who are you with? What has happened?	Emotions and body sensations What do you feel?	Your thoughts What do you think will happen? What are your concerns, fears? Be honest.	Managing anxiety Record the outcome of the anxiety episode. What have you done? How have you coped?

Make it future proof.

Have you learnt anything from this episode?
Have you discovered new coping strategies? Have you implemented them?

LET'S GIVE GRATITUDE!

List three things that you've enjoyed today or which made you happy, no matter how small. We need to see that even in the anxiety-filled days we have something to be thankful for.

1.

2.

3.

Anxiety record sheet

Date

Situation What are you doing? Who are you with? What has happened?	Emotions and body sensations What do you feel?	Your thoughts What do you think will happen? What are your concerns, fears? Be honest.	Managing anxiety Record the outcome of the anxiety episode. What have you done? How have you coped?

Make it future proof.

Have you learnt anything from this episode?
Have you discovered new coping strategies? Have you implemented them?

LET'S GIVE GRATITUDE!

List three things that you've enjoyed today or which made you happy, no matter how small. We need to see that even in the anxiety-filled days we have something to be thankful for.

1.

2.

3.

Anxiety record sheet

Date

Situation What are you doing? Who are you with? What has happened?	Emotions and body sensations What do you feel?	Your thoughts What do you think will happen? What are your concerns, fears? Be honest.	Managing anxiety Record the outcome of the anxiety episode. What have you done? How have you coped?

Make it future proof.

Have you learnt anything from this episode?
Have you discovered new coping strategies? Have you implemented them?

LET'S GIVE GRATITUDE!

List three things that you've enjoyed today or which made you happy, no matter how small. We need to see that even in the anxiety-filled days we have something to be thankful for.

1.

2.

3.

Anxiety record sheet

Date

Situation What are you doing? Who are you with? What has happened?	Emotions and body sensations What do you feel?	Your thoughts What do you think will happen? What are your concerns, fears? Be honest.	Managing anxiety Record the outcome of the anxiety episode. What have you done? How have you coped?

Make it future proof.

Have you learnt anything from this episode?

Have you discovered new coping strategies? Have you implemented them?

LET'S GIVE GRATITUDE!

List three things that you've enjoyed today or which made you happy, no matter how small. We need to see that even in the anxiety-filled days we have something to be thankful for.

1.

2.

3.

Anxiety record sheet

Date

Situation What are you doing? Who are you with? What has happened?	Emotions and body sensations What do you feel?	Your thoughts What do you think will happen? What are your concerns, fears? Be honest.	Managing anxiety Record the outcome of the anxiety episode. What have you done? How have you coped?

Make it future proof.

Have you learnt anything from this episode?

Have you discovered new coping strategies? Have you implemented them?

LET'S GIVE GRATITUDE!

List three things that you've enjoyed today or which made you happy, no matter how small. We need to see that even in the anxiety-filled days we have something to be thankful for.

1.

2.

3.

Anxiety record sheet

Date

Situation What are you doing? Who are you with? What has happened?	Emotions and body sensations What do you feel?	Your thoughts What do you think will happen? What are your concerns, fears? Be honest.	Managing anxiety Record the outcome of the anxiety episode. What have you done? How have you coped?

Make it future proof.

Have you learnt anything from this episode?

Have you discovered new coping strategies? Have you implemented them?

LET'S GIVE GRATITUDE!

List three things that you've enjoyed today or which made you happy, no matter how small. We need to see that even in the anxiety-filled days we have something to be thankful for.

1.

2.

3.

Anxiety record sheet
Date

| Situation
What are you doing? Who are you with? What has happened? | Emotions and body sensations
What do you feel? | Your thoughts
What do you think will happen? What are your concerns, fears? Be honest. | Managing anxiety
Record the outcome of the anxiety episode. What have you done? How have you coped? |
|---|---|---|---|
| | | | |

Make it future proof.
Have you learnt anything from this episode?
Have you discovered new coping strategies? Have you implemented them?

LET'S GIVE GRATITUDE!

List three things that you've enjoyed today or which made you happy, no matter how small. We need to see that even in the anxiety-filled days we have something to be thankful for.

1.

2.

3.

Anxiety record sheet

Date

Situation What are you doing? Who are you with? What has happened?	Emotions and body sensations What do you feel?	Your thoughts What do you think will happen? What are your concerns, fears? Be honest.	Managing anxiety Record the outcome of the anxiety episode. What have you done? How have you coped?

Make it future proof.

Have you learnt anything from this episode?

Have you discovered new coping strategies? Have you implemented them?

LET'S GIVE GRATITUDE!

List three things that you've enjoyed today or which made you happy, no matter how small. We need to see that even in the anxiety-filled days we have something to be thankful for.

1.

2.

3.

Anxiety record sheet

Date

| Situation
What are you doing? Who are you with?
What has happened? | Emotions and body sensations
What do you feel? | Your thoughts
What do you think will happen?
What are your concerns, fears?
Be honest. | Managing anxiety
Record the outcome of the anxiety episode.
What have you done?
How have you coped? |
|---|---|---|---|
| | | | |

Make it future proof.

Have you learnt anything from this episode?

Have you discovered new coping strategies? Have you implemented them?

LET'S GIVE GRATITUDE!

List three things that you've enjoyed today or which made you happy, no matter how small. We need to see that even in the anxiety-filled days we have something to be thankful for.

1.

2.

3.

Anxiety record sheet

Date

Situation What are you doing? Who are you with? What has happened?	Emotions and body sensations What do you feel?	Your thoughts What do you think will happen? What are your concerns, fears? Be honest.	Managing anxiety Record the outcome of the anxiety episode. What have you done? How have you coped?

Make it future proof.

Have you learnt anything from this episode?

Have you discovered new coping strategies? Have you implemented them?

LET'S GIVE GRATITUDE!

List three things that you've enjoyed today or which made you happy, no matter how small. We need to see that even in the anxiety-filled days we have something to be thankful for.

1.

2.

3.

The reflection corner

Please use this page to reflect on the last ten episodes.

Using free writing, look back, evaluate them, noting your "low points" (when you were stressed the most), whilst remembering to mention the "high", happy moments within the same timeframe.

My anxiety triggers

This page is for recording your anxiety triggers. Over the course of time, with the help of your anxiety records, you can identify situations in which your anxieties occur more often. Look for a pattern. Does your anxiety occur at the same time of day, maybe in the same location or situation; or when you around the same people?

1.

2.

3.

4.

5.

6.

7.

8.

Please use the next page if you need to list more triggers.

My anxiety triggers
(Continue on this page)

The reflection "station".

Let's pause for a moment and take stock; take a deep breath and look back.

Looking through your anxiety journal, identify the most common situations in which you experienced anxiety. Can you avoid these situations? Can you do anything to minimise the spike of anxiety in these situations?

Situation	Can you avoid it?	What can you do to minimise your anxiety related to this situation?

The power of positive thinking

To progress further, here is another exercise for you. Looking back through your log, find the thoughts that came to your mind while you were experiencing an anxiety attack, remembering what you were thinking. Remember how negative those thoughts were? Write them down here. Then, next to each, after looking back at the outcome of each situation and in particular at whether your fears have been fulfilled, please turn that negative and damaging thought into a positive thought.

For example: *I will fail at this test.* Did you get a 'fail'? *I only can do my best in this test.*

Negative thought	Was the thought fulfilled?	Positive thought

The future is bright!

Introspection is the informal reflection process, examining one's internal thoughts and feelings and reflecting on what they mean. It helps you to stay on the right path of self-reflection, asking "what" questions rather than "why" questions. "Why" questions can highlight our limitations and stir up negative emotions, while "what" questions help keep us curious and positive about the future (Eurich, 2017).

With this important point in mind, let's move on to the final questions and thoughts to evaluate the technique of anxiety journaling.

Have you learnt anything about your anxieties over the course of this journal? Have you discovered management techniques? Has the number of your overall (daily, weekly, monthly) anxiety episodes decreased?

No matter how small your victory seems at this time, record it below or use these prompt questions.

For example: Has there been progress? Did journaling help my anxieties? Do I understand my anxieties and their triggers? Do I see a pattern? Have I learnt to evaluate my fears? What have I learnt from anxiety journaling?

My anxiety and me

Drawing, doodling or using free writing technique, this is your space to express your relationship with your anxiety now.

Do you understand it better? Is it as dark and big as it was before? Do you know your triggers now? How can this knowledge empower you? Can you minimise the severity of your stress and anxiety attacks?

Reflect on the journal, on the work you have done and record it here.

Notes